I'M A VIKING!

A HISTORY BOOK ABOUT THE VIKINGS FOR KIDS

STORY BY C.J. ADRIEN
ILLUSTRATIONS BY CRYSTAL WHITHAUS

Copyright © 2021 by Christopher Adrien and Crystal Whithaus

All rights reserved. This book or any portion thereof may not be reproduced or used in any manner whatsoever without the express written permission of the publisher except for the use of brief quotations in a book review.

This is a work of fiction. Names, characters, businesses, places, events and incidents are either the products of the author's imagination or used in a fictitious manner. Any resemblance to actual persons, living or dead, or actual events is purely coincidental.

First Edition
Originally published in the United States in 2021 by Runestone Books
ISBN: 9798476653134

For more information, visit www.cjadrien.com

Hi.

I'm Leif.

And I'm a **Viking**!

Do you know what a **Viking** is?

Viking isn't something your **are**.

It's something you **DO**.

Such as....

Running

Swimming

A Viking is someone who goes on a **faraway adventure**. So when I say I'm a **Viking**, I mean it in the same way as someone who makes shoes might call himself a shoemaker.

"And, well, I'm not really a Viking. Not yet, anyway. **My dad** is the Viking of the family, and **I want to be just like him when I grow up!** He is also the chieftain of our village and has a lot of responsibilities.

Actually, he **works** most of the time. We hardly ever **play**.

Most **Vikings** live in the north, but our village is on an island in the south.

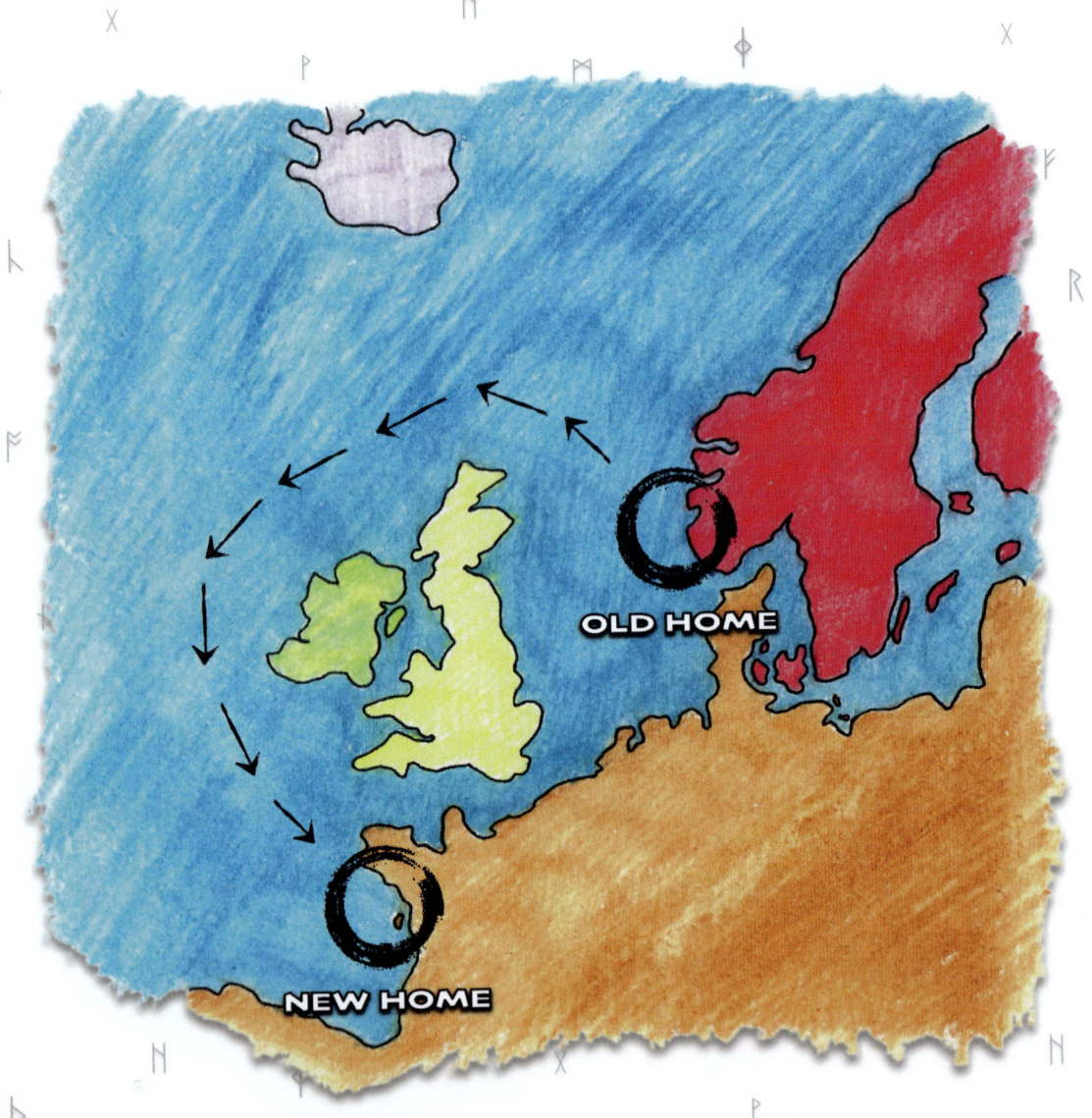

My dad and his brother had a disagreement over my grandfather's land, and my dad decided to move our family to **a new home**.

Of course, there were already people in our new home, so we **politely asked them to leave**.

Some days, my dad takes me on his ship to **teach me how to sail**.

"A true **Viking** is a **seafarer** first and a **warrior** second," my dad says. "His strength is his ship, not his **sword** or his **ax**."

Do you want to see our **ship**?

Our ship is named
Sail Horse of the Mountains of the Swans.

It's the **fastest** ship in Midgard!

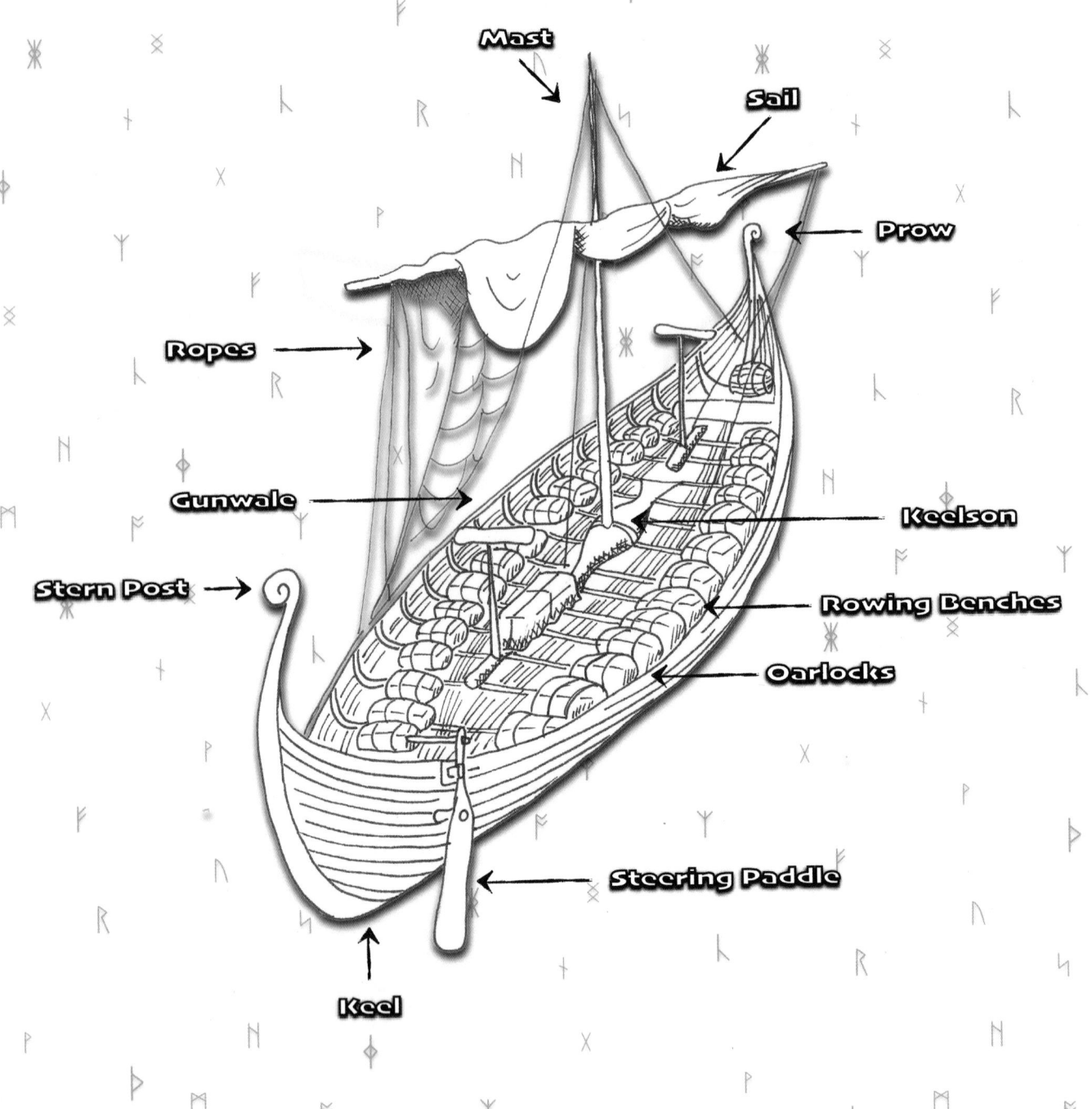

It has a **keel** and a **sail** so we can take it out to **sea**, but also a shallow draft so we can row up **rivers**.

Sailing is hard.

There are lots of **ropes** and lots of **knots** and I have a hard time remembering them all.

I'm still **too young** to follow my dad on a **long sea voyage**, so my dad always takes me home after a day or two.

The life of a Viking is pretty simple. In the **summer**, my dad leaves our home with **all his friends**.

BYE!

In the **autumn**, they return with lots of **gold** and **silver** and exciting stories about their **adventures**.

YAY!

My dad always remembers to bring something home for my brother Bjorn and me.

Last year he brought us two wooden **swords** from **France** that he says belonged to a **prince**.

When my dad comes home, he likes to throw big parties in our **great hall**.

We live in a great hall made of **wood and earth**, with **pillars** reaching for the **sky**.

My dad's parties always start with a **gift** to the **gods** to thank them for a safe voyage overseas.

An old woman called a **völva** decides what to sacrifice. They say she can **speak** to the gods and **understand** their will. Last time, she told my dad he had to offer **Odin**, the king of the gods, a **goat**.

My favorite god is **Thor**. He's the son of Odin and the **bravest** of all the gods.

He likes to fight giants (called **Jötunn**) with a hammer called **Mjolnir** and throw **lightning** bolts when he's angry.

My dad says we live in the realm of **Midgard**. The gods live in the realm of **Asgard**.

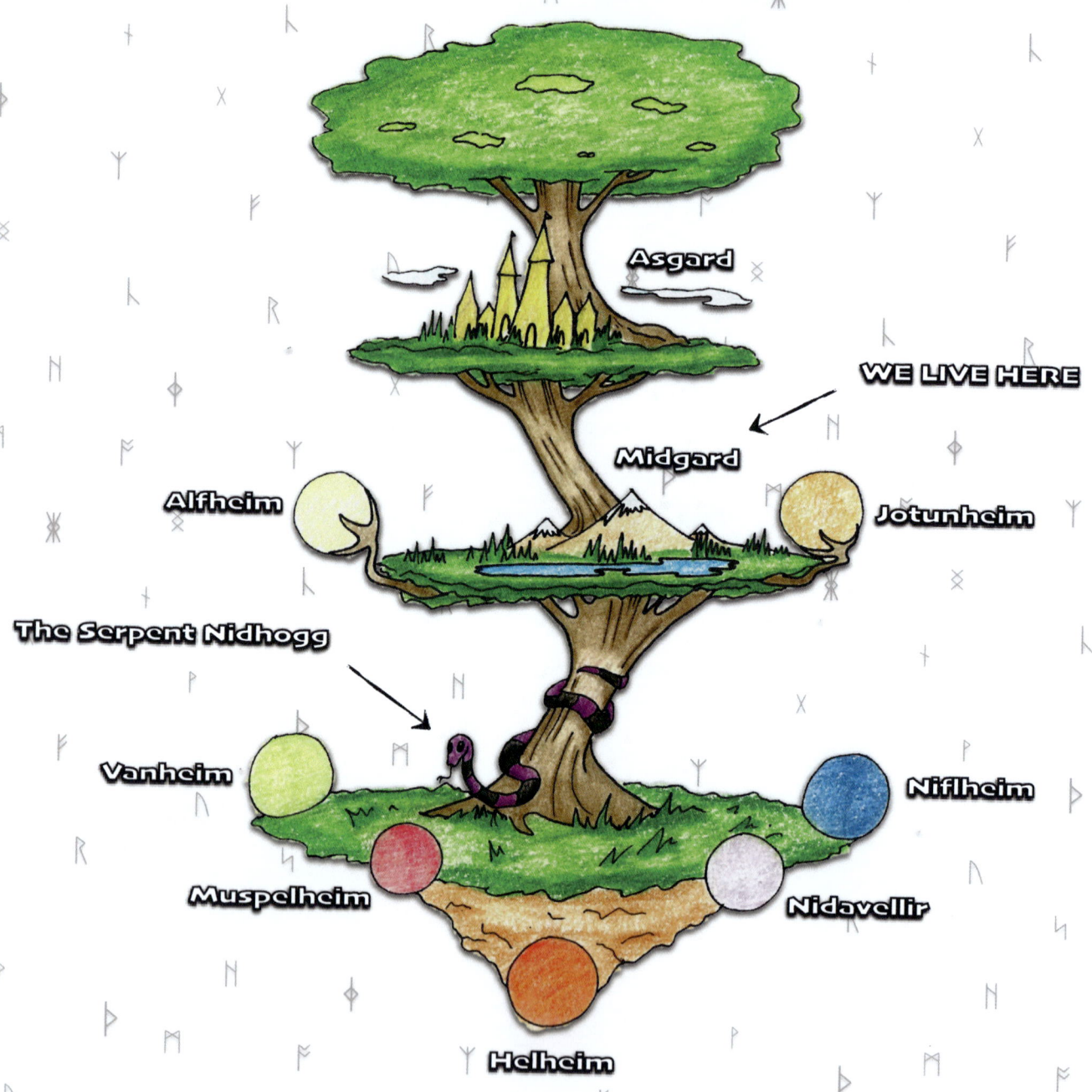

There are **nine** realms on the branches of the great world tree, called **Yggdrasil**, but I don't know much about all the other ones except that the **giants** live in **Jotunheim**.

A chieftain's son is expected to become a strong **warrior**. If I want to be a chieftain like my father one day, I have to be a great **fighter**, too.

My brother Bjorn and I **train** a lot together with the village **sword-master** Helge. My father learned from Helge when he was a boy and says he is the best **swordsman** in Midgard. Well, he's old now, so he was the best swordsman in Midgard.

When we're not training to be **sailors** and **warriors**, we like to play **games**. My brother Bjorn and I love to play **Hnefatafl**. Have you ever played it?

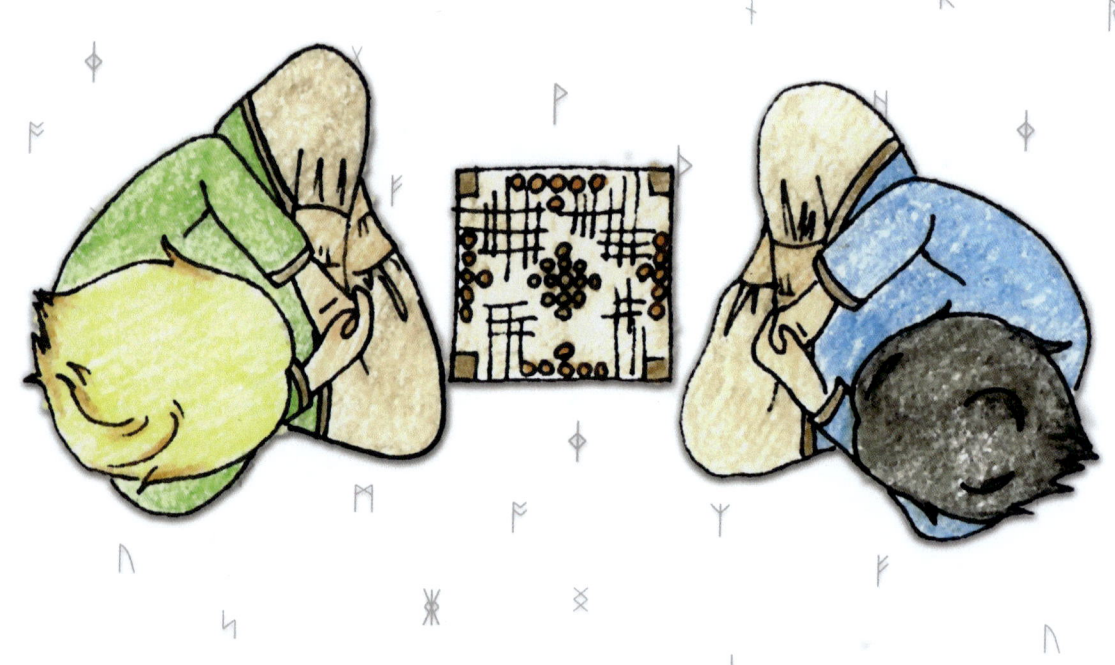

It's a strategy game played on a checkered board where two sides compete to take the other player's king piece. It's lots of **fun**! My dad bought me a set last time he visited the town of **Hedeby**.

My sister **Ingrid** doesn't like to fight or sail, but she does like many of the things my dad brings home for her.

She likes to play dress up with the **clothes** and **jewelry** my dad gives her.

One day a week, my mom says I have to **bathe**. I don't like it, but she says my dad does it, too, and if I want to be like him, I have to do it.

After washing, my mom **grooms** me with a **brush**, an **ear pick**, **tweezers**, and she trims my hair with **scissors**.

My **favorite** days are the ones where my dad comes to my room to tell me **stories** about his far-off **adventures** until I fall asleep.

I love hearing about the lands he **roves**.

I miss him when he's gone.

But, that's the life of a **Viking**. And that's what I want to be!

Printed in Great Britain
by Amazon